Dorothy Gates

Making Bedcovers, Duvet & Table Covers

with illustrations by the author

FREDERICK WARNE

FREDERICK WARNE
Penguin Books Ltd, Harmondsworth, Middlesex, England
Viking Penguin Inc., 40 West 23 Street, New York, New York 10010, U.S.A.
Penguin Books Australia Ltd, Ringwood, Victoria, Australia
Penguin Books Canada Ltd, 2801 John Street, Markham, Ontario, Canada L3R 1B4
Penguin Books (N.Z.) Ltd, 182–190 Wairau Road, Auckland 10, New Zealand

First published in 1985

ISBN 0-7232-3250-4

Printed in Great Britain by
Cambridge University Press

Contents

To my dear sister and brother-in-law
PAT and JIM.

Equipment List:

sewing machine
piping foot
zip foot
large square table (or floor space)
large sharp scissors
small scissors
sewing needles (assorted sizes)
tape measure
metre or yard stick
pins (sharp steel)
pencil
note pad
tailor's chalk

Materials Used:

fabric for item
lining
wadding
matching threads (40 gauge)
piping cord
touch and close tape

Important Note:

Metric conversions are approximate. Make sure you use either all-metric or all-imperial measurements; do not mix the two.

Introduction

There are many ways of covering a bed and of course our early ancestors were more concerned with warmth than with the appearance. Nowadays with better heating and the wide variety of fabrics to choose from, our main aim is to make the bed as distinctive as possible. It is, after all, the main piece of furniture in most bedrooms and therefore should be treated as the focal point.

Whilst the title refers specifically to bedcovers, I have also included details of headboard covers, duvets, pillow cases and bed drapes. These are all fairly simple to make, in their basic versions, and are well worth the effort.

Tablecloths are also included, as these can be used to cover bedside tables. When matched to the rest of the furnishings, they look very effective.

Throughout the book I have given the basic techniques for making each item, but these are all that are needed for you to be able to produce a limitless range of effects. The secret is in mixing and matching the different types of fabric, imaginative trimmings, etc. The whole character of a room can be changed by a new combination of colours and textures.

I do hope that the making of the things in this book give you great pleasure, and, particularly if you make a bedcover you will, at the end of the day, be able literally to 'rest on your laurels'.

D. G.

1 Bed Bases

When making the bed base the first thing to do is to measure the top of the actual base. Do *not* measure the mattress, as this will not be accurate, particularly if the mattress has spread somewhat with age.

Measure between the edge seams, or between the pipe lines if the base has been piped, then measure the depth of the base from the top edge to the floor. (Figure 1)

After measuring, estimate the amount of fabric to be used by making a cut-sheet. Assuming that the fabric is 122 cm. (48 ins.) wide, which is the average width of most furnishing fabric, the example of a cut-sheet used here is based on a single bed. If your bed is very much wider or longer, just use this cut-sheet as a guide, substituting your own measurements.

A bed base that is wider than the width of the fabric must have a join on either side, not down the middle, and this has to be borne in mind both when pattern matching and when joining the lining.

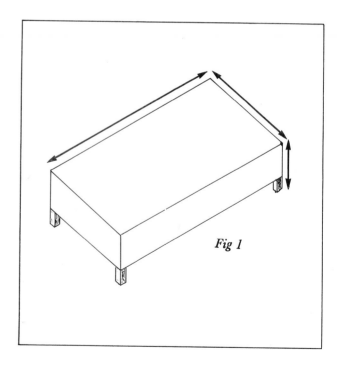

Fig 1

The Frilled Style

The frilled bed base is only frilled on the two sides and the bottom of the bed as most beds have a headboard or are set up against a wall. In order to keep the pattern on the base upright, the depth of the frill plus the turnings for the hem and joins must be cut out *across the width* of the fabric.

The pattern should be matched, if possible, but if it is an overall pattern – in the interest of economy – the frilled type *only* can be cut without matching.

The amount of fabric used for an average size bed base, with a gathered frill, is 3.50 metres (4 yds.) (single) and 4.50 metres (5¼ yds.) (double). This allows for strips of fabric to be placed on the lining used under the mattress. These strips of fabric not only strengthen the base but also prevent any sight of the lining when the top bedcover is removed. (Figure 2)

The amount of lining used will depend on whether or not you want to line the frill. If you are making the base in a washable fabric it would not need to be lined but if the fabric were very light or the top cover very heavy i.e. quilted, the weight would balance better with the base frill lined.

The following cutting plan will help you estimate and cut out your own size base. Add all the lengths together to find the total amount of fabric needed. The figures given are, of course, only for the purpose of an example. (Figures 3 & 4)

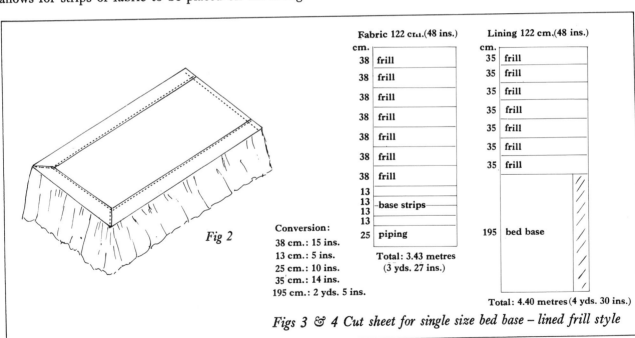

Fig 2

Conversion:
38 cm.: 15 ins.
13 cm.: 5 ins.
25 cm.: 10 ins.
35 cm.: 14 ins.
195 cm.: 2 yds. 5 ins.

Fabric 122 cm.(48 ins.)

cm.	
38	frill
38	frill
38	frill
38	frill
38	frill
38	frill
38	frill
13	
13	base strips
13	
13	
25	piping

Total: 3.43 metres
(3 yds. 27 ins.)

Lining 122 cm.(48 ins.)

cm.	
35	frill
35	frill
35	frill
35	frill
35	frill
35	frill
35	frill
195	bed base

Total: 4.40 metres (4 yds. 30 ins.)

Figs 3 & 4 Cut sheet for single size bed base – lined frill style

The sizes marked on the cut-sheet are the actual cut sizes and turnings of 1.25 cm. ($\frac{1}{2}$ in.) and 4 cm. (1$\frac{1}{2}$ ins.) have been allowed for the hems.

The Kick-pleat Style

The cut-sheet for this style is calculated in the same manner as the frilled base. To find how many widths of fabric will be needed to go round the three sides of the bed, first measure the length and add 20 cm. (8 ins.). Now measure the width of the bed and add 20 cm. (8 ins.). Finally add the length of the bed plus 20 cm. (8 ins.) for the third side. Add these lengths together and then work out how many widths of fabric it will take to cover this length. (Figure 5)

Make out a cut-sheet to calculate the amounts. The kick-pleat style must have a pattern match and is also better lined as it will hang straighter.

Cutting out – Both styles are cut in the same manner.

Cut the base lining first, allowing turnings and a 4 cm. (1$\frac{1}{2}$ ins.) hem at the head end.

Cut the widths of lining for the frills or kick pleat.

Measure and cut the frill or kick-pleat widths in the fabric, matching the pattern if there is one.

Cut the side strips.

Assembling the frilled base – Pin all the widths of frill fabric together, selvedge to selvedge, to form a long length. Repeat this with the lining.

Join all these widths together by machine, open the seams and press flat. (Figure 6)

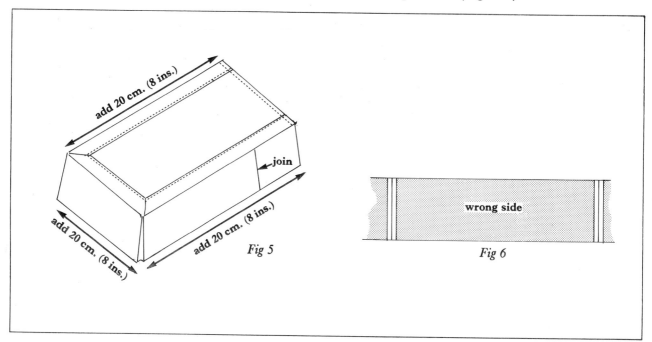

Fig 5

Fig 6

Place the two lengths with right sides together and pin along the bottom, leaving the 1.25 cm ($\frac{1}{2}$ in.) turning.

Machine along the pin line.

Press the turning down towards the fabric and fold the lining back until the top edges are level. This will leave a 2.5 cm. (1 in.) piece of fabric showing on the lining side.

Press along the bottom edge to make a fold and place a few pins along the top edge to stop the frill from twisting. (Figure 7)

If the frill is to be gathered a simple method is to use the zigzag stitch on the sewing machine as follows:

Using a length of strong twine, lay the twine along the top of the frill and secure the end by winding it round a pin. Zigzag over the twine in a straight line just down from the top edge. (Figure 8)

Sew the whole width of frill in the same way and then put it to one side until the base top is ready.

The base top – Very few bases are absolutely square on the corners so cut a curve on each of the four corners of the lining.

Turn the hem allowance over at the top edge, turn the raw edge under and machine across. (Figure 9)

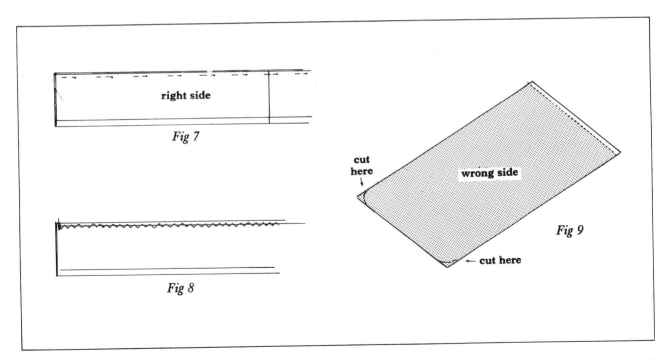

right side

Fig 7

Fig 8

cut here

wrong side

cut here

Fig 9

9

Join the widths of fabric already cut into strips to fit the two sides and place the other strip along the bottom edge of the width.

Pin into position, so that the edges meet, and then place the right side of the lining to the wrong side of the fabric. (Figure 10)

Where the fabric crosses at the corner, fold back to form a mitre. (Figure 11)

Leaving a 1.25 cm. ($\frac{1}{2}$ in.) turning, trim back and fold one section over the other section so that they make a pair.

Sew the inside of the strip in place with a top stitch, then top stitch down the mitres. Round the corners off to match the lining. (Figure 12)

If you wish to pipe the base, this is the stage to make and apply the piping. To do this, fold the piece of fabric across the grain and cut along the fold. Cut off strips 4 cm. ($1\frac{1}{2}$ ins.) wide. (Figure 13)

To join the piping, place the two pieces together, right sides facing, to form a right angle. Sew across this angle and continue joining all the pieces in the same way. (Figure 14)

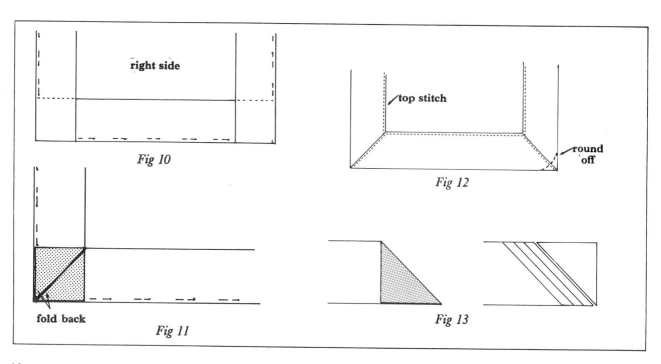

Fig 10

Fig 11

Fig 12

Fig 13

When you have a long enough length to fit right round the bed base, trim the joins back to 1.25 cm. ($\frac{1}{2}$ in.) and open the turnings so that they lie flat.

Place a length of cord in the centre of the piping, fold it down its length and stitch along the length just near enough to hold the cord in place – but not *too* close at this stage – using a zip foot on the machine. (Figure 15)

Piping the base – To pipe the base, start at the top corner, turn the ends of the piping under to neaten them and pin in place all round the three sides. Keeping the raw edges of the piping to the raw edge of the base, stitch fairly close to the piping. (Figure 16)

Fitting the frill – Measure the frill along its length and place a pin at the half-way mark. Now take the measurement from the half-way mark to the end and halve this, inserting pins as before. You have now halved and quartered the frill.

Now do the same on the bed base. Measure the three sides and then halve and quarter this measurement, marking each point with a pin.

Gather the frill up to fit between the marks and pin into position. (Figure 17)

Take the end of the frill just round the corner at the top end to enable the base to clip on neatly and help prevent it from slipping.

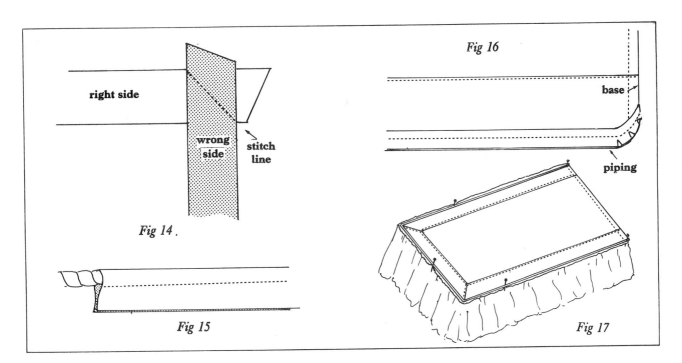

right side

wrong side stitch line

Fig 14.

Fig 15

Fig 16

base

piping

Fig 17

Place the top of the base to the frill when machining so that you can follow the machine line already there from the line of piping. Machine inside this line, so that the cord is caught tightly between the fabric. (Figure 18)

Keep the gathers evenly distributed, easing a few more gathers into the corners so that they do not pull out of shape. (Figure 19)

When the machining is finished, turn the frill back out of the way and trim the cottons and any untidy edges on the turnings. Using a zigzag stitch, sew round the edge of the turning to neaten. If you do not have a zigzag stitch on your machine, work another line of machine stitching near the edge of the turning and this will stop the edges fraying. (Figure 20)

Kick-pleat base – The kick-pleat base is made on exactly the same lines as the frilled base. The top of the base is prepared with the strips added and the pleat is lined in just the same way, although you will see from the cut-sheet that the pieces of the pleat are cut to size, plus the allowance to make the inverted (or kick) pleat on the corners. 10 cm. (4 ins.) has been allowed at each end of the width and the lengths, giving a total of 20 cm. (8 ins.) to fold under at the bottom corners and 10 cm. (4 ins.) at the top corners. (Figure 21)

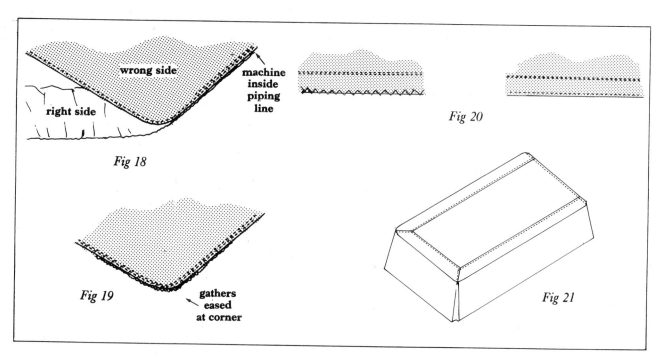

Fig 18

Fig 19

gathers eased at corner

Fig 20

Fig 21

Halve and quarter the base and the kick pleat and pin in place, starting with the centre mark on the sides. When you have pinned to within 15 cm. (6 ins.) of the corner, start again from the centre of the bottom and work out towards the corners again. (Figure 22)

The excess material will now be at each corner; fold this into a pleat, making sure that the join is not going to be visible from the front – it is better to have slightly more turning on one side of the pleat than to let the join show. (Figure 23)

On the top edge, one pleat only is sufficient; the rest of the fabric can be turned just round the corner.

Machine the pleat section all round on to the base, in the same way as the frilled base, and neaten.

To prevent the base from slipping about under the mattress, a double tape can be sewn on at each corner, long enough to tie round the legs or casters; this is a great help when turning the mattress. (Figure 24)

There are several variations of styles of bases – a box pleat is very attractive, for example. From the basic techniques in this chapter, you will be able to decide for yourself which variation will be most suitable for the fabric you wish to use and the style of the room, using the making-up methods given.

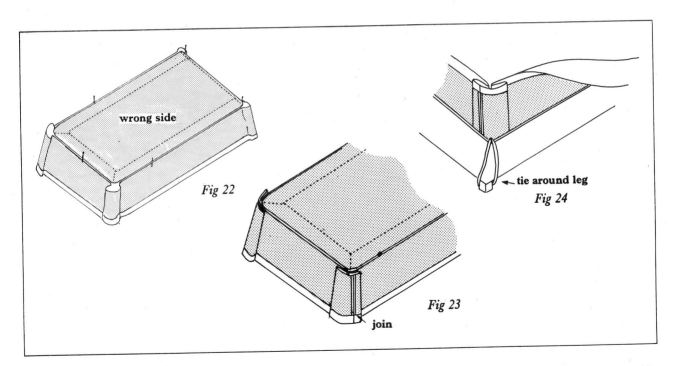

wrong side

Fig 22

join

Fig 23

← tie around leg

Fig 24

2 Throwover and Frilled Bedcovers

Measuring and Estimating

Having made the bed base, you will now want to make a bedcover to go over the bed. The simplest type is a throw-over style. If you do not have a base cover, the bedcover usually comes to about 1.25 cm. ($\frac{1}{2}$ in.) off the floor all round but as a bed base cover has already been made it must be visible. The bedcover, therefore, should cover the top of the base by approximately a quarter of its depth. Measure from this point, over the bedclothes, to the corresponding point on the other side. Then measure from top to bottom of the bed in the same manner, leaving at least an extra 15 cm. (6 ins.) to tuck down behind the pillows. (Figure 25)

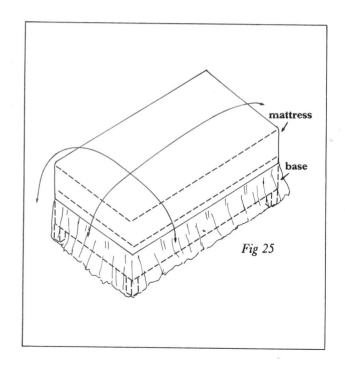

mattress

base

Fig 25

The bedcover for a single bed can usually be cut from two widths of fabric for a single size and three widths for a double size for the floor-to-floor cover. Two widths will be enough for a single or double size, however, if it is only to cover part of the base. (Figures 26 & 27)

The strip of fabric wasted at the side of the single bed can be used as a frill or trimming for pillow cases, or it can be used up in the base frill if the same fabric is being used for both.

Matching Patterns

This is an important part of the measuring as allowance must be made for the pattern repeat when the fabric is patterned. Measure the length required and add turnings – 10 cm. (4 ins.) if unlined and 8 cm. (3 ins.) if lined – to your overall size. Measure the width and again add the turnings.

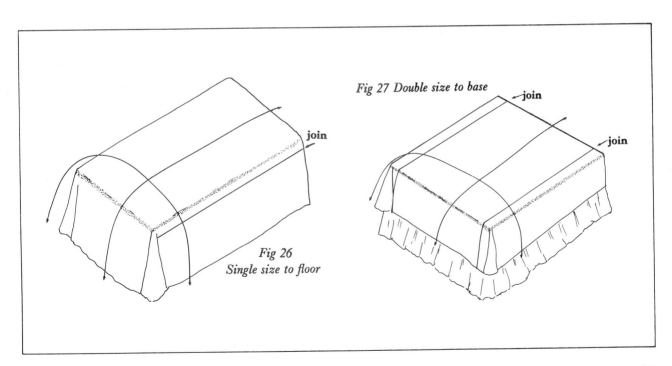

Fig 27 Double size to base

join

join

join

Fig 26
Single size to floor

Now cut off the first length, following the pattern across. If the fabric has a very large pattern, make sure that the centre of the pattern is positioned in the centre of the bed – bouquets of flowers look very strange if they become headless when the bedcover is tucked in at the top.

Having cut the first length, place the next piece of fabric alongside it, selvedge to selvedge, and move it into position until it matches. Pin the edges together and then cut to size. (Figure 28)

The two widths for a single size bedcover have now been cut. Place the two lengths together, right sides facing (Figure 29), and then – keeping the selvedge edges level – fold back the top fabric until the pattern matches. Make a crease along this line, fold the fabric back and pin along the crease line. The fabric should match perfectly when you stitch down this line. (Figure 30)

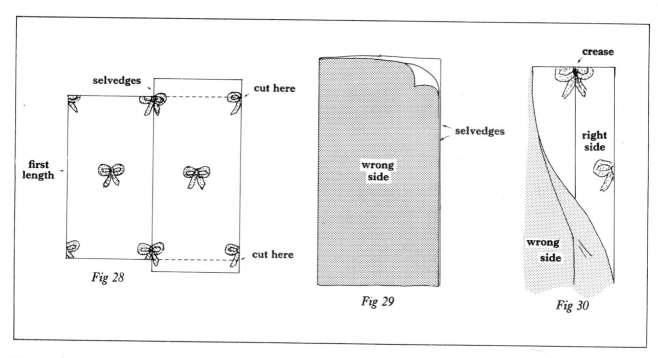

Fig 28

Fig 29

Fig 30

Join the fabric on the other two selvedges in the same manner. You will now have a tube of fabric. (Figure 31)

Fold this down the centre of the width and smooth the fabric out flat on a table. Measure half the finished width, across from the centre, including the turnings. Cut to size. (Figure 32)

To round the corners at the bottom edge so that they do not dip when they fall over the edge of the bed, measure from the centre fold half the width of the actual bed, *including bedclothes*. Place a pin to mark this measurement. (Figure 33)

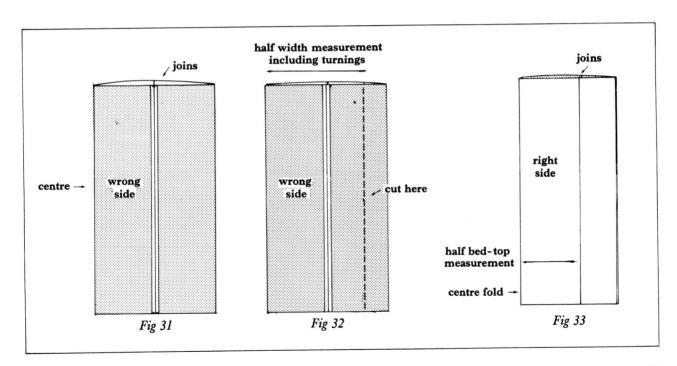

Fig 31   *Fig 32*   *Fig 33*

Measure to the outside of the cover that you have just cut and measure the same amount up from the bottom of the fabric. Mark with a pin where these two measurements meet in from the side and bottom. (Figure 34)

Then, using a rule, keep one end on the mark and gradually move the rule in a semi-circle, marking the measurement on the fabric as you go. (Figure 35)

Cut round this line, making a nice curved edge. This will ensure that the corners will fall in an even fold level with the rest of the finished bedcover.

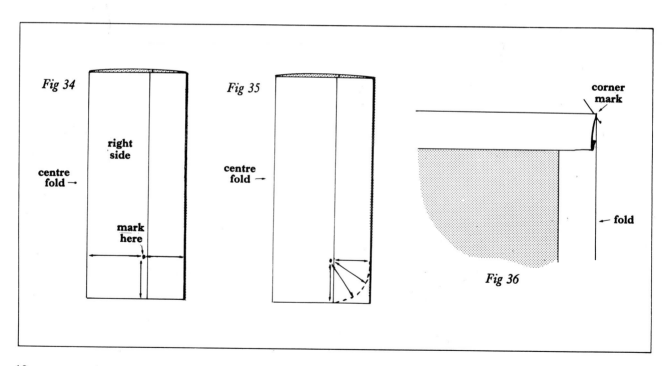

Unlined Bedcovers

This type of throw-over bedcover can be unlined. It is easy to wash and ideal for cotton or light-coloured fabrics that need frequent laundering. It is also suitable for heavy-weave fabrics that do not need to be lined to give them body.

Turn the raw edge in 1.25 cm. (½ in.) and then another 2.5 cm. (1 in.). Pin along the straight edge at the top first until you are about 15 cm. (6 ins.) from the corner. Fold the hem up to the corner and then fold the side hem in place, creasing it well so that you can see the actual finished corner, and mark this point with a pin. (Figure 36)

Take the point of the corner of the fabric and turn it under 1.25 cm. (½ in.).

Fold the corner over at the point where the pin marks the outer edge. (Figure 37) Push the excess fabric equally each side into the edge fold, turn under the raw edges and you should have a nice flat mitred corner. (Figure 38)

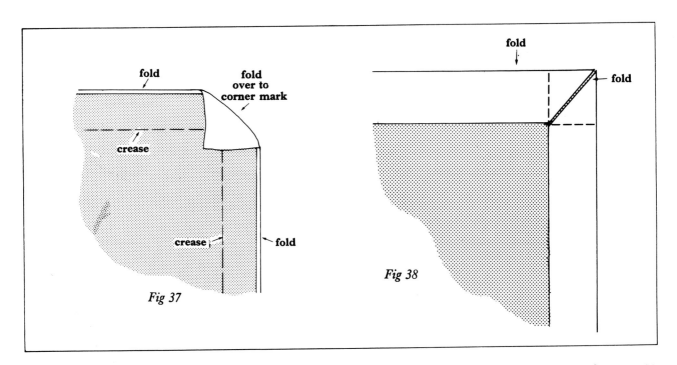

Fig 37

Fig 38

Turn the sides in and continue all round until you meet the top corner again, mitre this corner and pin across to meet the first pins.

The bedcover can now be machined all round with a matching thread. The rounded corners will have to be eased in as you sew; if the folded edge is pinned on the fold it will avoid making points as you turn the corner. (Figure 39) The stitching should sweep round in a continuous curve. (Figure 40)

If you prefer the stitch line to be invisible, then the hem can be slip-stitched all round by hand. (Figure 41)

Another alternative is to sew a fringe on the bedcover with the fringe covering the stitched hem.

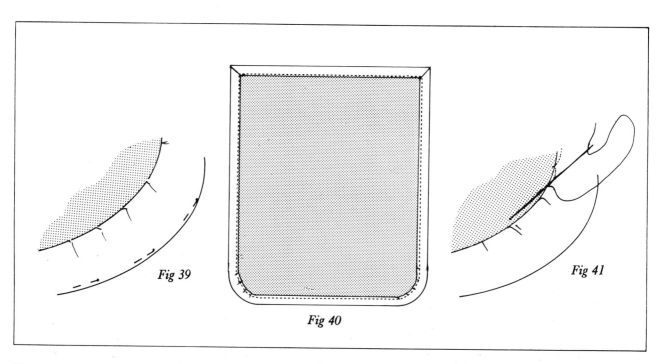

Fig 39

Fig 40

Fig 41

To make the fringe appear heavier, it is a good idea to sew it on so that the bottom edge is level with the bottom of the bedcover. (Figure 42)

If you are rather short of fabric, the fringe can be used to lengthen the bedcover by using the minimum turning and sewing the head of the fringe to the lower edge of the bedcover.

This time, however, neaten the edge by turning the raw edge to the right side of the fabric, place the head of the fringe so that it just covers it and work two lines of machine stitching so that the raw edge is completely held in place and covered by the fringe. (Figure 43) This method can also be used if you want to use a braid instead of a fringe for edge trimming. (Figure 44)

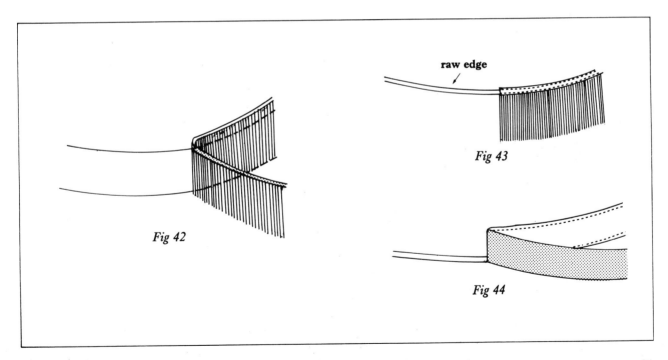

raw edge

Fig 43

Fig 42

Fig 44

An embroidery stitch is a neat way to finish the hem as it gives a slightly stiff and heavy edge. By using a contrasting shade it can be a main feature, picking up the colour of the furnishings in the room. Try a piece of stitching on an odd scrap of fabric to make sure that the pattern of stitching is even; when you are satisfied, start stitching in the middle of the top of the bedcover, and try to finish with the design following on at the end. (Figure 45)

Stitch on the machine hem line and then stitch two more rows at intervals of 0.7 cm. ($\frac{1}{4}$ in.) either side of the line.

Another way of finishing the edge is to bind it in a contrasting or matching colour. To bind the edge, cut strips of fabric across the cross-grain of the fabric to give maximum stretch. (Figure 46) Whatever width you decide the binding will be showing on the front, add the same amount at the back plus 3 cm. (1 in.) for turnings.

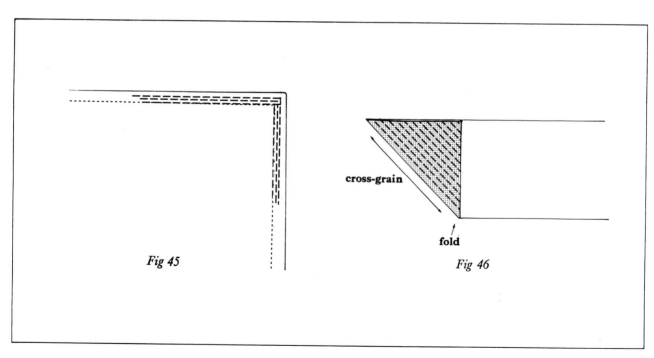

cross-grain

fold

Fig 45

Fig 46

Cut enough strips to go all round the bedcover, allowing enough extra for joins.

Join the strips across the diagonal as piping. (Figure 47)

Open them out and trim to a 1.25 cm. ($\frac{1}{2}$ in.) turning. (Figure 48)

Place the strip, right side to right side of the bedcover. Keeping the edges level, start in the middle of the top edge and pin the binding 1.25 cm. ($\frac{1}{2}$ in.) in as you reach the square corner, making a pleat of 1.25 cm. ($\frac{1}{2}$ in.) to allow the fabric to turn the corner without dragging. (Figure 49)

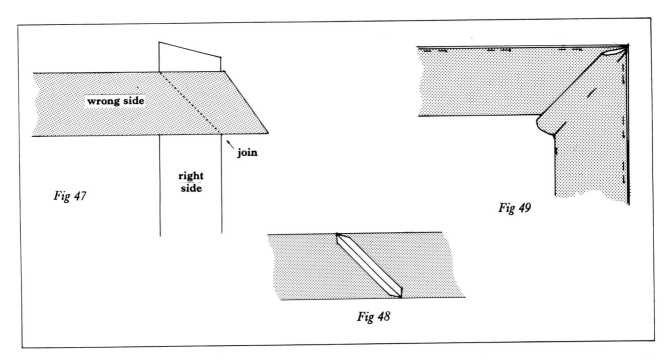

wrong side

join

right side

Fig 47

Fig 48

Fig 49

Continue to pin all round the bedcover and, when you get back to the beginning, allow about 7.5 cm. (3 ins.) to overlap. (Figure 50)

Machine all round the pin line, tacking first if you prefer to do so, and stop machining at the overlap. (Figure 51) Pin the fabric so that it meets and lies flat on the bedcover. Trim to 1.25 cm. (½ in.) and turn the two pieces so that they join diagonally. (Figure 52)

Continue to stitch to the bedcover. (Figure 53)

Fold the binding over the edge and, turning in the raw edge 1.25 cm. (½ in.), pin along the stitch line so that it just covers it. (Figure 54)

Using a matching thread, slip-stitch all round the bedcover so that the binding is held firmly in place. (Figure 55)

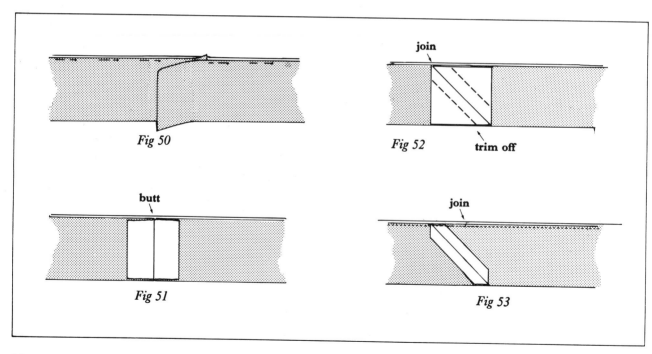

Fig 50

Fig 52   trim off

join

butt

Fig 51

join

Fig 53

Fitted Bedcovers

If you decide you would rather have a fitted bedcover here, again, are a few basic styles to choose from. So much depends on the fabric you use, whether the bedcover has a base you wish to show and if you want it to have a tailored look or a pretty frilled effect.

The basic shaped bedcover, with a piped edge and frill, is made and cut out in the same way as the bed base. The only difference is that, instead of a lining for the top, the main fabric is used and at least 15 cm. (6 ins.) allowed to tuck over at the head of the bed. (Figure 56)

Follow the instructions for the bed base up to the point where the base is trimmed at the edges and finished off in zigzag stitch.

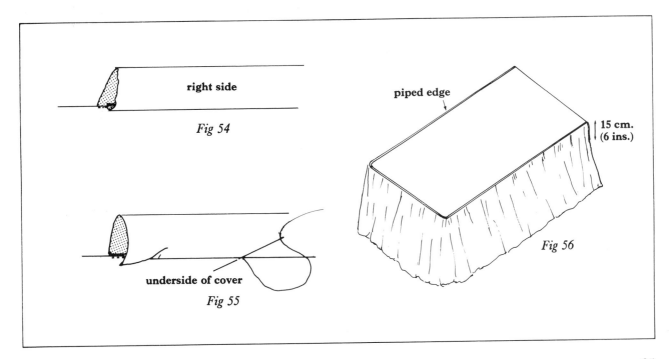

right side

Fig 54

underside of cover

Fig 55

piped edge

15 cm. (6 ins.)

Fig 56

25

The top of the bedcover must be lined so that all the edges are hidden neatly inside.

Cut a length of lining the same size as the bedcover top plus the previously recommended allowance for turnings. Then, with the wrong side facing the table, spread the bedcover right out and turn the frill in so that it lies on the right side of the top with its edges exposed. (Figure 57)

Measure and mark with a pin the centre of the bottom edge, the centre of the top edge and the centre of the sides of the bedcover. Now do the same operation with the lining. (Figure 58)

With the right side of the lining facing the right side of the fabric, line the centres up and, starting at the centre bottom, pin from each centre mark towards the corners, easing the lining along rather than pulling it tight. If it is pinned in tight, by the time it is machined it will be too tight and will drag against the top cover.

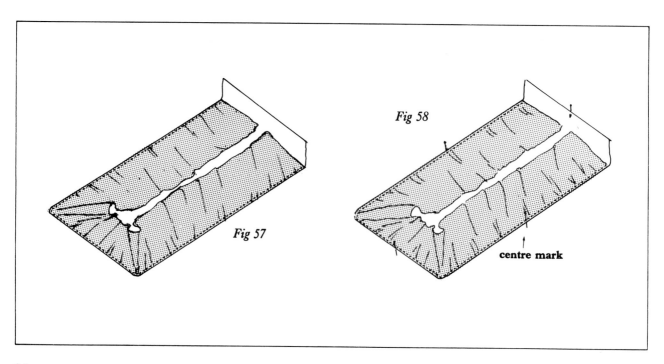

Fig 57

Fig 58

centre mark

This is why it is necessary to work from each centre mark as this ensures that the lining does not twist and therefore prevents dragging.

Starting at the centre top, machine all round, leaving a gap at the top of approximately 40 cm. (16 ins.). (Figure 59) Trim any odd ends of cotton away and then turn the bedcover right side out. Turn in the turnings in the gap and slip-stitch together.

Press to remove any creases and the bedcover is complete.

The plain kick-pleat style of bedcover can be made by following the method used for the base and then lining it in the same way as the frilled bedcover.

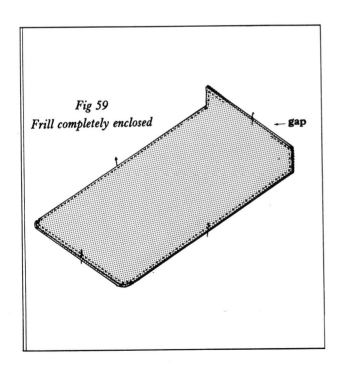

Fig 59
Frill completely enclosed   ← **gap**

3 Quilted and Scalloped Bedcovers

This type of cover is, of course, very luxurious and looks very glamorous with its scalloped edges. It can be made in almost any fabric whether patterned or plain, cotton or silk, depending on the type of room in which it is to be used.

The price, too, must be taken into consideration as there is not only the fabric to be bought but also the padding for the quilting and the lining as well.

Quilting can be purchased by the metre (yard), and this is fine if you do not have to join it to make up the width. If it is joined after it has been quilted it tends to be bumpy and the stitch lines will not always line up.

If you are sending the fabric to a specialist firm to be quilted, it is a good idea to join all the lengths you require first. An extra allowance of 3 cm. (1 in.) to every 30 cm. (12 ins.) is the usual allowance as the fabric tends to shrink when quilted. If, however, you decide to do it the hard way and quilt it yourself, you will get a great deal of satisfaction from the finished article. (Figure 60)

If you have never done quilting before, it would certainly be too ambitious to outline-quilt all round a design on an ordinary domestic machine. I therefore describe the basic method of quilting in diamonds which you can adapt to suit your fabric.

Preparing the Fabric

First the fabric must be cut to size, allowing for the take-up on the quilting and turnings so that you have plenty of fabric. If the fabric needs to be joined, this should be done before anything else.

The fabric has to be joined in widths for the scalloped edge in order to keep the pattern upright. To calculate how many widths will be needed, measure round the bed on both sides and along the bottom. There must be a centre width at the bottom; if there is not an odd number of widths, therefore, one will have to be cut in half and added at either end.

Cut the depth of the deepest part of the scallop, add turnings and take up allowance. Cut and join all the pieces first. (Figure 61)

Now cut and join all the lining pieces.

Finally cut the length of padding to be used and butt the edges together. In most general use now is a polyester wadding as it is washable and dry cleanable. If you want a thick quilt, one layer of 4 oz.-wadding will be sufficient. For a less padded effect, one layer of 2 oz.-wadding will be adequate. Try the wadding under the fabric and place a few pins through to give an idea of how it will look.

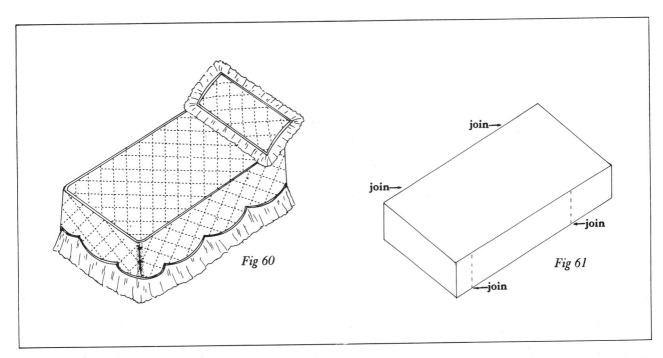

Fig 60

Fig 61

To join the wadding, butt the two edges together and oversew right through the thickness. Do not pull the thread tight or a ridge will form. The stitches should hold it together so that it will not part when going through the machine. (Figure 62)

Once you have prepared the fabric, press the joins open and place it on the padding, wrong side down. Tack a line right down the centre length and another line across, using a large loose stitch about 10 cm. (4 ins.) long.

Tack down and across at intervals of about 30 cm. (12 ins.) until the padding is secure. (Figure 63)

Now tack the padding to the side pieces so that they will be ready to quilt after you have finished the top. (Figure 64)

Quilting in Diamonds

One of the most straightforward yet effective methods of quilting is in diamond shapes.

Having decided on the size of the diamonds, make a gauge with a piece of card or use the quilting guide on your machine, if it has one. To start the quilting, measure 30 cm. (12 ins.) up from the lower left-hand corner and mark with a pin. From the same corner,

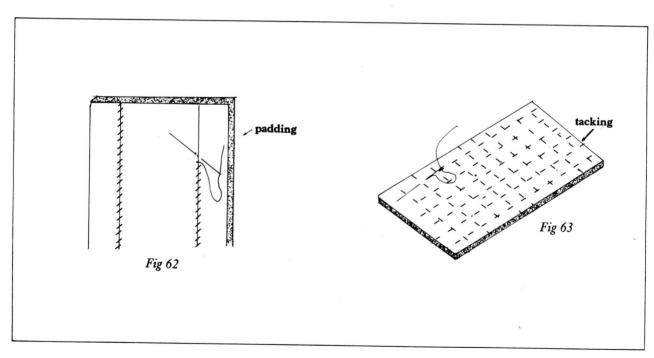

padding

Fig 62

tacking

Fig 63

measure 30 cm. (12 ins.) across the width and mark as before. Now place a rule from one mark to the other, across the fabric, and mark this line with tacking stitches in a bright colour. (Figure 65)

The angle which you start is of great importance. It does not matter if you start higher or lower up the quilt so long as you measure an equal distance from the corner. If you do not do this the diamonds will eventually run completely out of square when they are crossed with the other lines.

Start machining across the line, using a fairly large stitch to counteract any dragging underneath. Hold the fabric at the back and front of the foot and guide it through evenly.

You will have more bulk to push through the machine as you progress across. To make it easier to handle, roll the quilt as small as possible to enable it to pass under the machine head.

Keep the quilting running in the same direction. Do *not* be tempted to turn it round and start the other end because, if you do, it will cause a twist in the quilting and spoil it.

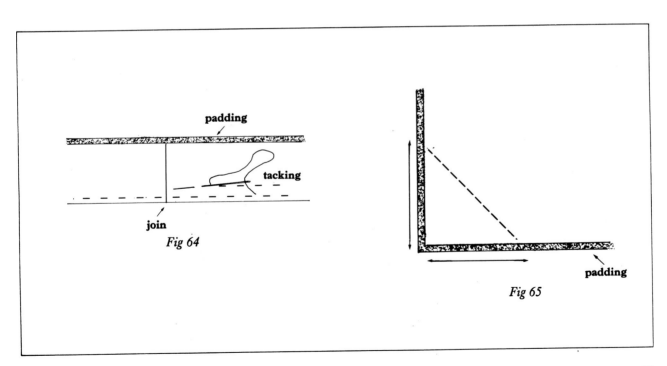

Fig 64

Fig 65

Continue across the quilt until all the stitching is complete one way. Now turn the quilt round and measure in from the opposite corner, as before, to get the correct line to start. (Figure 66)

Machine across the first lines, keeping the fabric taut so that there are no pleats at the point where the two lines of stitching meet. (Figure 67)

Having completed the quilting on the main bed-cover you can now start on the side pieces, remembering to get the starting angle correct. (Figure 68)

Quilt all the side section and then the whole thing can be cut to size.

You may find that the quilting has not stayed exactly square; if this is the case, ignore the quilting lines and cut the top *square* because otherwise it will not lie flat on the bed.

Keep the quilting flat and do not try to stretch it out at all.

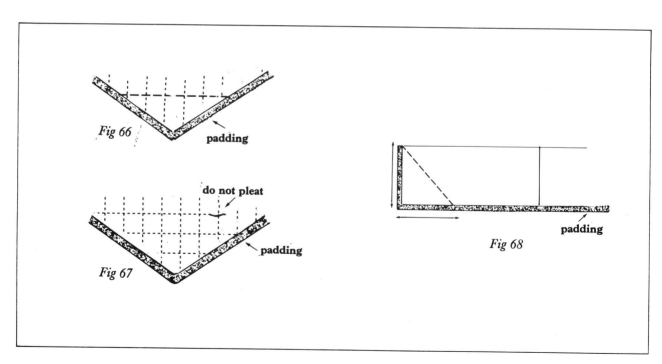

Fig 66   padding

do not pleat

Fig 67   padding

Fig 68   padding

Measure the size carefully and allow turnings of 1.25 cm. ($\frac{1}{2}$ in.) on each side and at the top and bottom. Cut with large, sharp scissors.

Now cut the side pieces to size but do not cut the scallops yet. (Figure 69)

Scallops

The scallops have to be worked out to fit the size of the bed; on a single bed there would usually be one whole scallop in the middle of the bottom and one at each corner. It is not a good practice to have the narrow part of the scallop on the corner as it looks much better wrapped round at this point. (Figure 70)

The shortest depth of the scallop should cover the mattress and bedclothes while the deepest part should be approximately two-thirds of the depth from the top of the bed to the floor. If it is any deeper it will look top-heavy. (Figure 71)

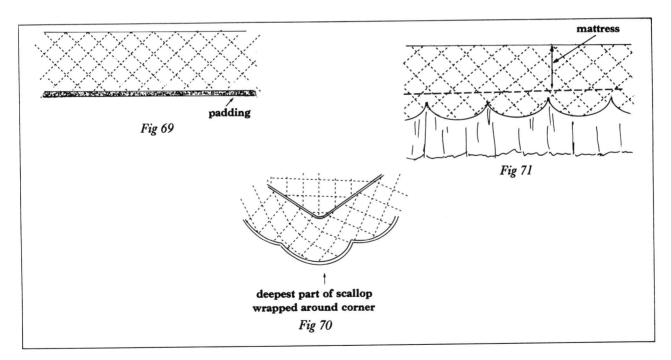

padding

Fig 69

mattress

Fig 71

deepest part of scallop
wrapped around corner

Fig 70

Decide the size of scallop you want and allow turnings top and bottom. Make a template with a piece of card or buckram to the size of your scallop and place it along the edge of the quilting, starting in the centre of the bottom edge. (Figure 72)

Draw round the template with a sharp pencil or chalk. When you are almost at the end of the quilting, where it fits to the top edge, let the last scallop go straight from the centre so that it can finish square at the end rather than on a short upturn. (Figures 73 & 74)

When you have cut out all the scallops, make up enough piping, in a matching or contrasting fabric, to go all round the edges of the scallops and all three sides of the top of the bedcover.

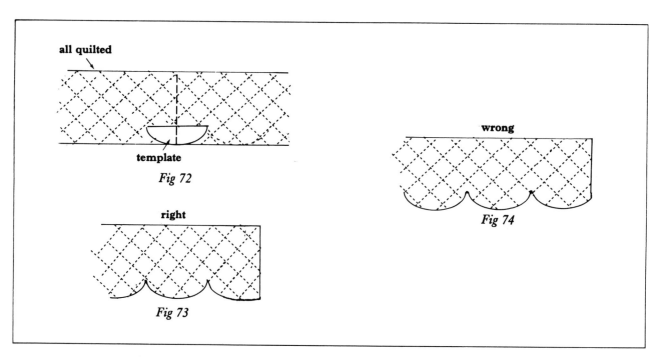

Fig 72

Fig 73

Fig 74

Measure along the sides of the bedcover the exact measurement of the bed, adding 1.25 cm. (½ in.) for turnings at the bottom, and mark the length with a notch on both sides. These are the points from which the scalloping is joined. Slightly round the corners at the bottom edge and mark each corner with a notch. (Figure 75) The top is now ready to receive the piping.

Cut the last 1.25 cm. (½ in.) of cord out of the piping and turn the fabric under to make a neat start and finish. (Figures 76 & 77)

Pin the piping 1.25 cm. (½ in.) in from the end, starting at the top of the bedcover. Pin all round, clipping the piping at the rounded bottom corners and finishing at the top edge, using the same method as at the start.

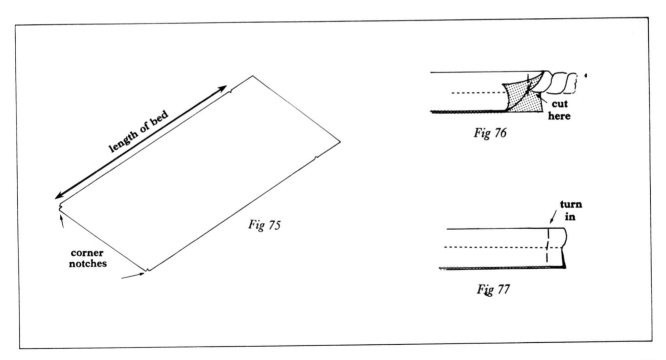

length of bed

corner notches

Fig 75

cut here

Fig 76

turn in

Fig 77

Having piped the top, the scallops can now be piped. Start at the top edge and continue down the end and round all the curves. When you reach the point of each scallop, clip the piping right to the point to make the sharp turn. (Figure 78)

Continue to pipe all the way round, finishing at the opposite top corner.

Lining the Scallop

The lining must be done very carefully as it must not be tight or it will pull the scallops out of shape.

Place the lining, wrong side down, on the table and mark the centre with a pin. Find the centre of the scalloping and place the two pieces together. Pin out from the centre along the line of piping but do *not* cut the lining to the shape of the scallops yet as this will be done after they have been machined.

Machine inside the stitch line, from the padded side, as this will enable the lining to remain slack. (Figure 79)

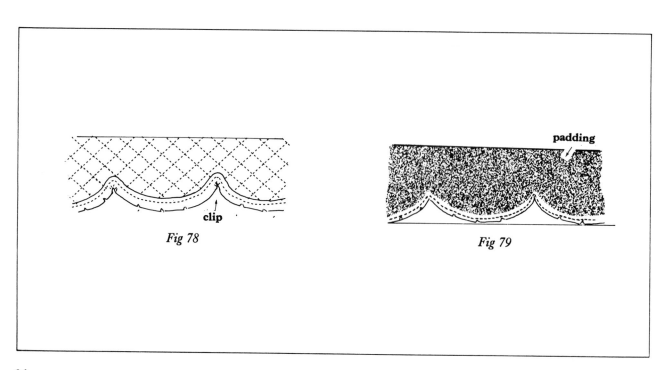

Fig 78

Fig 79

When all the scallops have been machined round, trim round the lining to match the padding, snipping along the rounded edges and into the points of the scallops. (Figure 80)

Turn right side out, pushing the turnings out so that the scallops are smoothly rounded.

Pin the lining and quilting together at the top edge, keeping the lining upright, and then tack along the top edge to keep the lining from moving. (Figure 81)

To assemble the bedcover, pin the centre bottom of the bedcover top to the centre of the scalloped length. With right sides facing, pin in opposite directions until the end of the scallops reaches the notch at the top of the bed. With the top uppermost, and still using the piping foot, machine as close to the piping as you can.

Check that you have a clean line of piping all round.

Now place the bedcover, wrong side down, on the table and line it in as described on page 26.

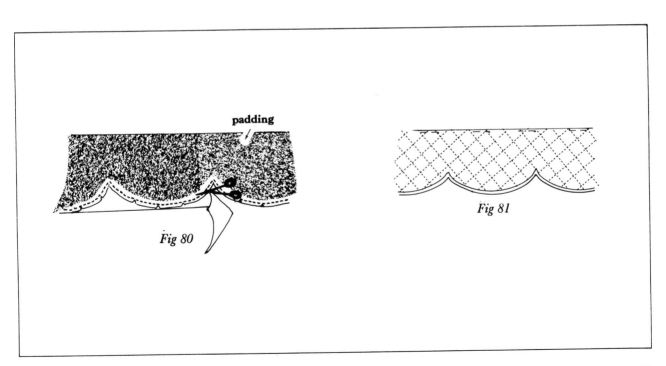

padding

Fig 80

Fig 81

4 Frilled Pillows

Having finished the bedcover, a frilled pillowcase to match will complete the picture. Most of the methods used have already been described in the previous text and so I will give the basic method only.

Quilt enough fabric to make a pillowcase for an average sized pillow. You will need one piece of the exact pillow size and one piece 15 cm. (6 ins.) longer, plus turnings and take-up allowance. (Figure 82)

Cut the pieces of quilting to the required sizes – the extra piece is to be used as the pillow flap.

Cut three pieces of lining to the same size as the quilting and prepare these sections of lining now, so that you can get on with the assembly of the pillowcase without any interruption.

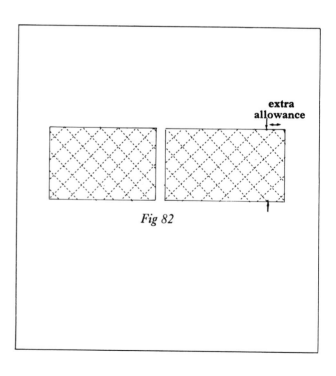

extra
allowance

Fig 82

Place the back piece of quilting, wrong side up, with the lining under it so that their right sides are together. (Figure 83)

Pin along the short edge, taking in the turning allowance.

Machine across and then fold the lining right back so that the wrong sides are now facing.

Tack several rows of stitching across to hold the lining and quilting together. (Figure 84)

Line the pillow flap in the same way, only turning in one end and leaving the other sides raw. (Figure 85)

Now place the lining to the front piece of quilting, wrong sides facing, and make several lines of tacking to hold them together.

From now on, all the lined pieces should be treated as a single piece of fabric.

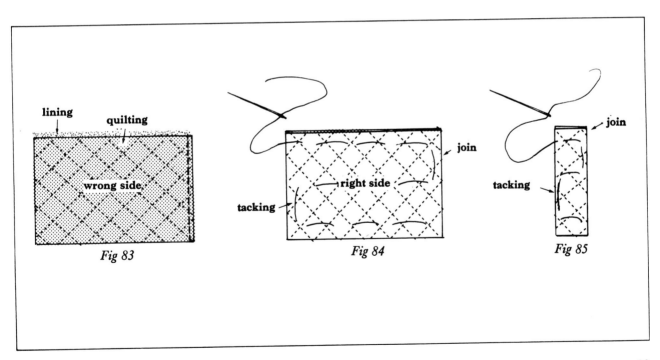

Fig 83   Fig 84   Fig 85

Measure round the outside of the front piece of quilting and make enough piping to go right around the edge. If you piped the bedcover in contrasting piping, do the same on the pillow.

Pipe the pillow all round on the front piece and then measure around the edges again for the frill which will need at least double the measurement. Cut strips 15 cm. (6 ins.) deep, join them together to form a circle and fold down the centre length. (Figure 86)

To gather the frill, use the method described on page 9.

Divide the frill into quarter measurements and do the same on the piece of quilting. Mark the sections with pins and then gather each quarter of frill to fit into the quarter marked on the pillow section, keeping all the raw edges together.

Ease a little extra fullness into the corners so that they will fall flat when turned back. (Figure 87)

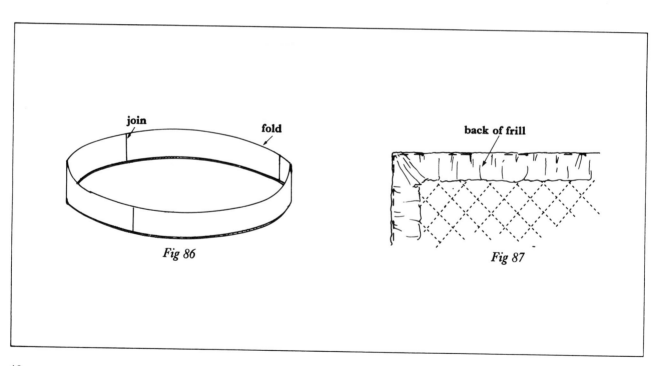

Fig 86

Fig 87

When the frill has been sewn all round on the front side, join the pillow flap to the front piece of the pillow, making sure that it pairs with the opening on the back, i.e. both patterns should be upright when the pillow is finished.

Place the flap right side to right side of the pillow-case, enclosing the frill in between. (Figure 88)

Machine as close to the piping under flap as possible, starting right at the raw edge and machining across. Turn the flap back out of the way temporarily. (Figure 89)

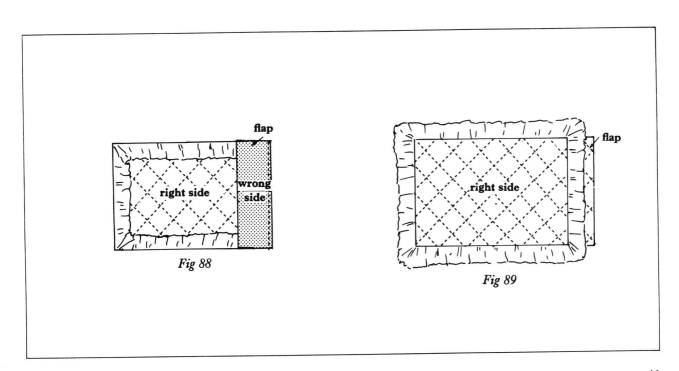

Fig 88

Fig 89

Place the front piece to the back piece, right sides facing, and then, from the wrong side of the front piece, pin all round the three edges, leaving the flap free. Machine all round as close to the piping as possible. (Figure 90)

Turn the flap over the top of the pillow to the back piece so that it encloses the opening and machine down the two sides of the flap, thus attaching it to the seams at the side. (Figure 90A)

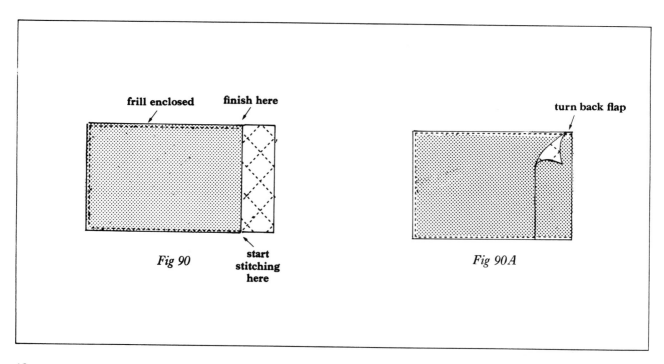

Fig 90

Fig 90A

Trim the seam allowances all round and zigzag over the edges so that the seams are neat. Pull out all the tacking and turn the pillow right side out. (Figure 91)

Slip a pillow into the case, tucking the corners under the flap and into the bottom corners so that the case is well filled out. (Figure 92)

The covered pillow will just add the finishing touch to the bedcover.

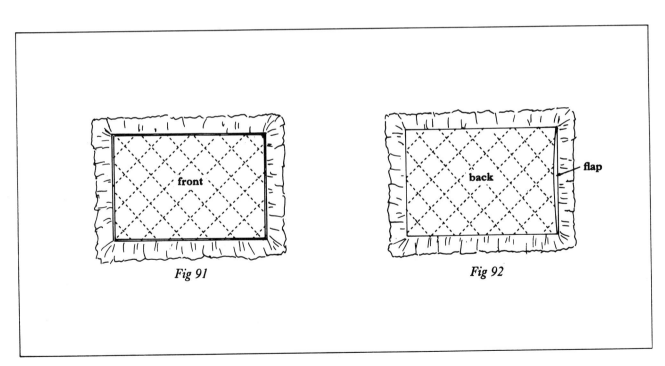

Fig 91

Fig 92

5 *Duvet Covers*

Because most people find it uneconomic as well as extremely messy to make their own duvet, they prefer to buy a ready-made one and then make different covers for it.

If you have not already got a duvet, and are thinking of buying one, the following are some points to look for:

The duvet should consist of a row of channels with the filling in between each channel, evenly distributed. If the duvet does not have a gusset between each channel you will not have the insulation you should expect from a duvet. (Figure 93)

Buy the best you can afford, bearing in mind that if you spill anything on a down or feather duvet it will have to be dry cleaned, whereas man-made fibre-filled duvets can be washed.

Try to buy one *at least* 60 cm. (24 ins.) wider than your bed size. If you do not have at least this much overhang you will find that you have lost your duvet in the night and only the floor will be kept warm.

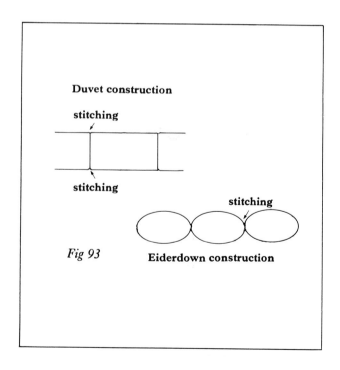

Duvet construction

stitching

stitching

stitching

Fig 93   Eiderdown construction

The length for an average sized bed should be at least two metres (6 ft. 6 ins.), again allowing for an overhang at the end of the bed which also keeps your feet warm.

If you have an old eiderdown that you wish to make into a duvet there are many manufacturers who make cases ready to fill. This is usually a better proposition than making the case yourself.

The best way to fill a duvet case is to hang it on a clothes line with two pegs in each channel. (Figure 94)

Fill one section at a time and pin the opening together immediately. Once all the sections have been filled, turn the raw edges in, pin in place and machine two rows of stitching along the edge.

This completes the duvet and the cover can now be started.

Duvet Cover with Piped Edge

To make the outer cover you will need sufficient fabric to cover both sides of the duvet, for the piping and a little extra to match the pattern if necessary.

For the closure you can use a zip, hooks and eyes, press studs or touch-and-close tape. The length of closure needed is a third of the length of the duvet. (Figure 95)

Personally, I like the opening in the side as it is less inclined to be handled when in use but many covers are made with the opening at the bottom edge.

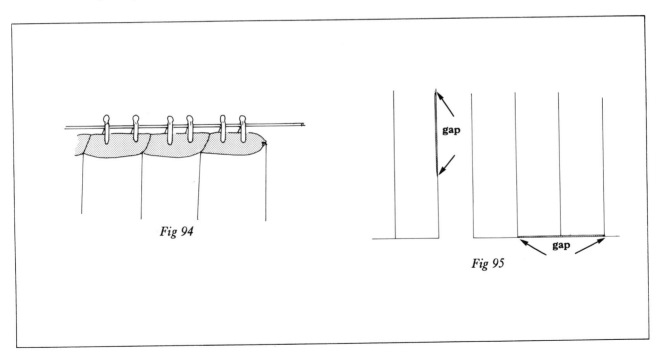

Fig 94

gap

gap

Fig 95

Measure the length and width of your duvet and add turnings of 1.25 cm. (½ in.) all round.

Cut the first length and match the pattern as on page 16. The width of fabric will be in the centre and, if it needs a join, this must be put on either side. (Figure 96)

Cut the front to size first and then the back.

Cut strips of piping (see page 10) and make up enough length to go all round the duvet, allowing for joins.

Starting in the middle of the bottom edge, pipe all round and join up at the starting point.

Insert a pin to mark each end of the opening which must be centred exactly in the side of the cover.

Machine as close as you can to the piping in the area between the pins. If this is not done, the opening will have a thicker piping than the rest of the duvet. (Figure 97)

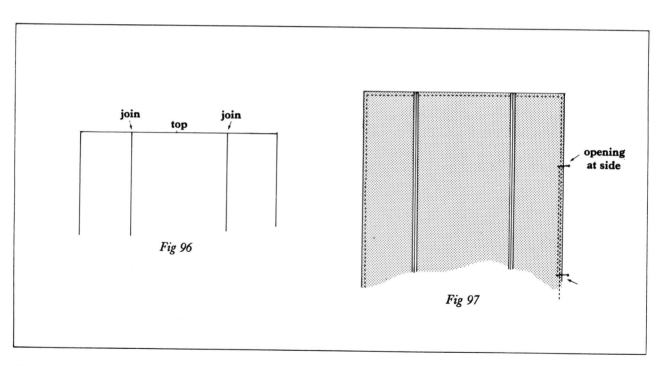

join   top   join

Fig 96

opening at side

Fig 97

If you are using a touch-and-close tape, sew one half on now between the pins. (Figure 98)

Find the exact position on the back of the duvet and sew the other half of tape on to it, placing the right side of the tape to the right side of the fabric which will then turn back without any stitches showing. (Figure 99)

Pin the rest of the cover together and machine all the way from the start to finish of the opening. (Figure 100)

Sew across the ends of the tape to neaten the closure. (Figure 101)

Trim all the edges of the turnings and neaten with a zigzag stitch or another row of stitching near the edge.

To keep the duvet into the corners of the cover, make a loop of tape on the cover at each corner and sew a double tape on each corner of the duvet; now tie the corners tightly while the cover is still inside out. (Figure 102)

Finally turn the whole thing the right way round and complete by closing the opening. The duvet is now ready for use.

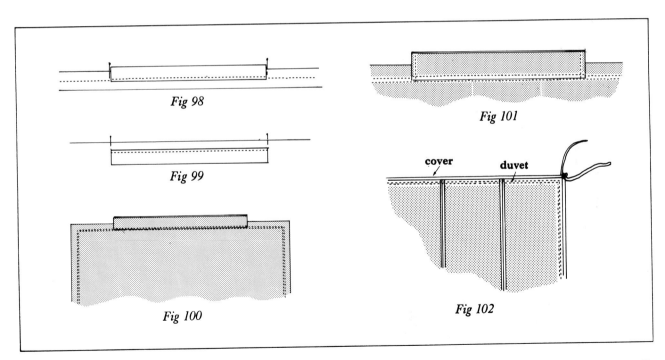

Fig 98

Fig 99

Fig 100

Fig 101

Fig 102

6 *Loose Covers for Headboards*

If you already have a headboard for your bed the chances are it will not now match your new bedcover. You may have considered having it re-upholstered but – if it is in good condition and the padding is sound – a loose cover could be the answer. The main advantage of a removable cover is, of course, that it can be taken off for washing or dry cleaning. As headboards come in a variety of shapes, I have described the most basic type and this can easily be adapted to fit your own shaped board. (Figure 103)

This type of board has a thickness at the top edge of about 4 cm. (1½ ins.). Only the front and the border around the edge need to be covered in fabric; the back can be covered in lining.

Measure from the top centre to the bottom edge of the board, adding 1.25 cm. (½ in.) at the top for turnings and 4 cm. (1½ ins.) at the bottom for a hem.

Measure across between the widest points and add a 1.25 cm. (½ in.) turning on either side.

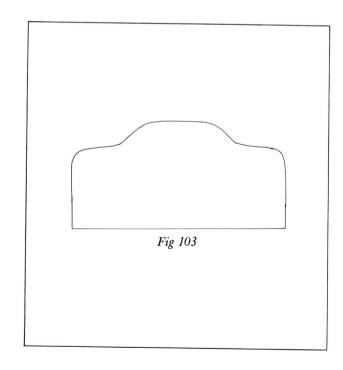

Fig 103

Measure the border from front to back and add 1.25 cm. ($\frac{1}{2}$ in.) turnings on either side, then measure it from the bottom edge, up and over the board to the other side, and again add a 4 cm. ($1\frac{1}{2}$ ins.) turning for a hem on either side.

If the fabric is not wide enough for the board, a piece must be matched and joined on either side of the centre width. The border must also be matched in the same way as the pattern has to be matched on either side to give it enough width.

Secure the fabric to the front of the board with a few pins. Line the border up in the centre so that the pattern, if any, runs straight and pin out from the centre. Take the turning only on the border but follow the outline of the board with the front fabric. (Figure 104)

Pin all round and then, using a piece of lining for the back, repeat the same process, keeping the outline clear and making sure you have not twisted the border.

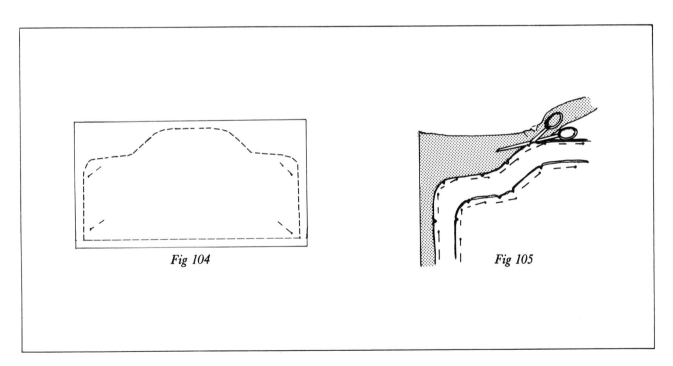

Fig 104   Fig 105

Trim the front and the back down to the same size turning allowance as in the border, cutting several notches into it as you go. (Figures 105 & 106)

Unpin all the pieces, measure up enough piping to go along both sides of the border and make up the two lengths ready to use (pages 10–11).

Start piping the border 3 cm. (1¼ ins.) from the end, graduating off to nothing. Finish in the same way at the end. Turn the cover round and pipe the other side. (Figures 107 & 108)

Matching the notches on the border and the front section, pin the two pieces together, with right sides facing.

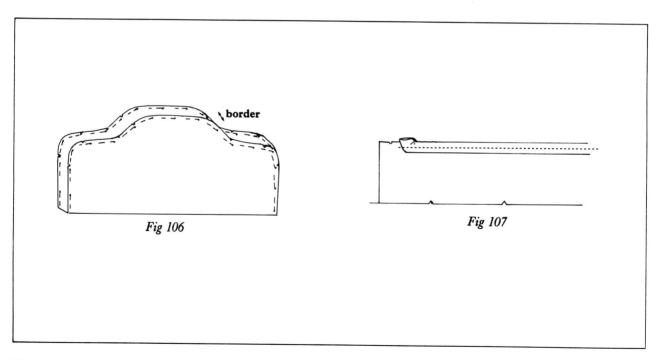

Fig 106

Fig 107

Machine from the bottom edge right round to the other edge, keeping as close as possible to the piping.

Repeat the same process with the back lining so that the cover is now assembled. (Figure 109)

Trim the turnings and neaten them by **zigzag** stitching on the edge or by making another row of stitching.

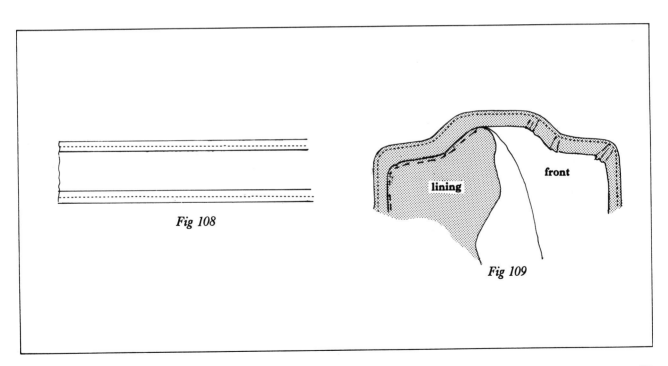

Fig 108

Fig 109

Now fold up the hem allowance, turn under the raw edge and hem all round. (Figure 110)

To keep the cover from slipping, a length of tape approximately 15 cm. (6 ins.) can be sewn at intervals along the bottom edge. Four pieces will usually be sufficient; match them up on the back so that they tie underneath the board. Tie down tightly in a bow and tuck the ends up into the cover. (Figure 111)

You will notice that there is no opening on this cover. This is because it is the same size all the way down and it will therefore slip over and pull down.

If, however, the headboard is wider at the top than at the bottom you will need an opening in the side in order to get the cover on. (Figure 112)

This opening can either be made with touch-and-close tape (see page 47) or, of course, hooks or press studs may be used.

If you want the opening to be completely invisible, the lining can be split down the middle at the back and hemmed on each piece. In this case, allowance for the extra turnings must be made when cutting the lining.

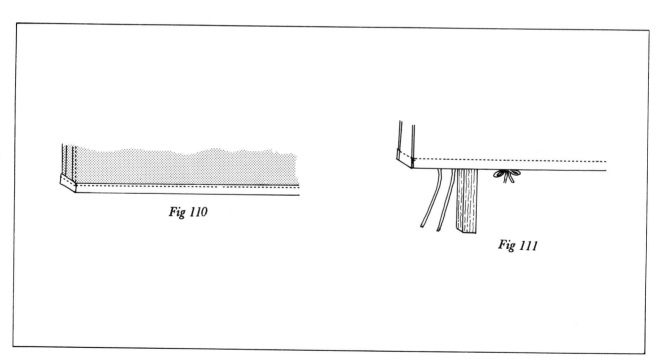

Fig 110

Fig 111

The lining should be overlapped at the top and caught in with the border.

Sew tapes to both sides of the opening and tie together when the cover has been fitted on to the board. This has the great advantage of allowing the fabric some leeway if the cover shrinks a little in the wash. (Figure 113)

You can, of course, use any of the other methods of closure described previously.

In fitting the cover over the headboard, open it out and fit both sides evenly on the top edge, pulling down both sides together, if you can, but if not just ease it down on either side, keeping it level, to prevent any splitting or stretching.

Once the cover is on and all the ties are in place, turn the piping to face in one direction as this gives a much straighter and cleaner outline.

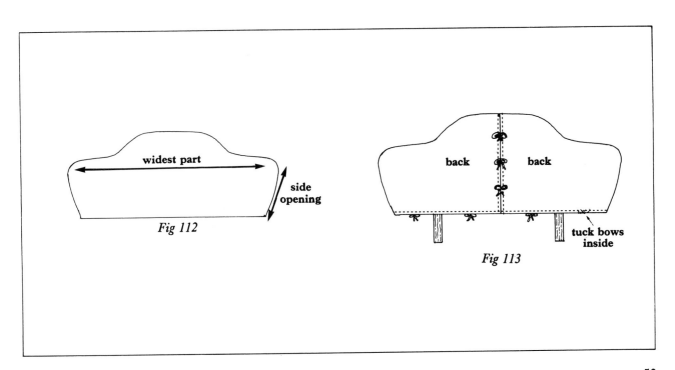

Fig 112

Fig 113

7 *Table Covers*

You may wonder why tablecloths should be included in this book. The reason is that the humble tablecloth has now become a table cover and is used quite frequently nowadays on a table at the side of the bed which replaces the more traditional bedside cabinet.

The Round Table Cover

The amount of fabric used for a round table cover is quite surprising; it is nearly always more than you would guess so it is wise to measure the table carefully before buying the fabric. This is done by measuring from the floor to the top edge, across the table centre and down the other side. The diameter is the most difficult measurement as it must be exactly midway across the table and unless this has a centre join there is nothing to guide you. (Figure 114)

The answer is, of course, to take a template of the top with a piece of newspaper by placing it on and pencilling round the edge. Cut out the template, fold

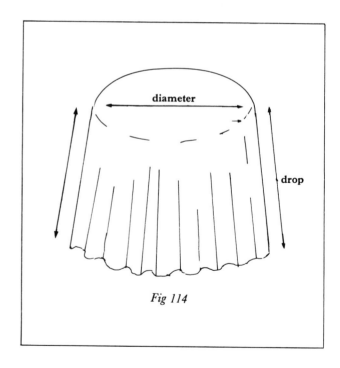

Fig 114

it in half and put it back on the table. The centre fold will be the exact diameter, providing the template you have made fits perfectly. (Figure 115)

The measurements you have just taken are the finished size so an allowance must be added on both sides for a hem; an extra 4 cm. (1½ ins.) on each side is usually sufficient.

You now have the length but, unless you have been very lucky and have found the right width fabric, you will have to join a piece on either side to make up the width. If you are using 122 cm. (48 ins.) fabric and your table measures anything up to 230 cm. (90 ins.), you will need two widths of fabric; anything over that measurement will not allow for joins and hem turnings and so you will need three widths.

The table cover in this example is 230 cm. (90 ins.) plus the hems and so the finished cut size is 238 cm. (93 ins.) after it has been joined. This is shown in the following cutting plan using two lengths of 238 cm. (93 ins.) joined at the selvedge edges and cut down the centre of the width.

Now fold the main width down the centre lengthways and mark the centre point with a pin. (Figure 116)

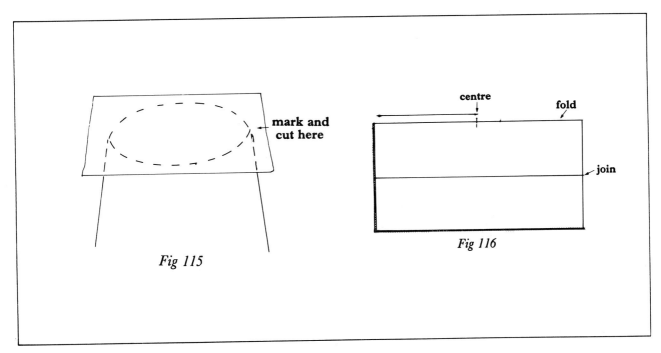

mark and cut here

centre

fold

join

Fig 115

Fig 116

Make sure that the fabric is lying as flat as possible and then, starting from the centre pin, measure half the cut measurement 119 cm. (46½ ins.) out towards the edge. Go all round at intervals of 15 cm. (6 ins.) marking a line of chalk or using pins until you have half a circle marked. Now cut along the marks and the table cover is ready to sew. (Figure 117)

You can, of course, fold the fabric in four instead of in half which saves half of the marking out. If you use this method, however, you must take great care that the fabric is flat or you will not get a true circle. (Figure 118)

It is possible to save some fabric if you work out on the cutting plan where the first join will start. The amount you save will be from this point to the outside edge of the fabric which, when doubled – as it is – may be worthwhile. It may well be a good idea to work out beforehand exactly what the saving would be. On the whole, however, the waste pieces can be used to trim or pipe the edges or be put to good use at a later date. (Figure 119)

The cover can now be finished plain with a hand slipped hem or it can be finished in a number of other ways.

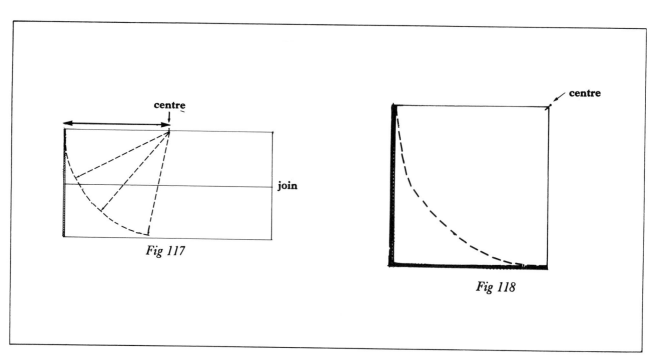

Fig 117

Fig 118

The Plain Hem

Turn the allowance up and press to make a firm crease, then turn in the raw edge and slip stitch all round. The fabric will pleat slightly in a few places as you progress round. Try to keep the pleats as flat as possible, making them a little smaller and closer together, where necessary, to avoid any sharp turns.

If you are going to add a fringe it will not be necessary to sew by hand as the machine stitching will be covered. I have described various finishes for bedcovers and any of these can, of course, be used on a table cover. There are a few more, though, that are particularly suitable for table covers.

Frilled Edge

A frilled edge at the base of the cover makes it hang well as the weight holds the folds in place.

To make a frill, measure all round the base (circumference) of the table cover, work out how many widths of fabric will be needed to go round it and then double the number of widths. If the fabric is very fine, up to three times the circumference may be used. (Figure 120)

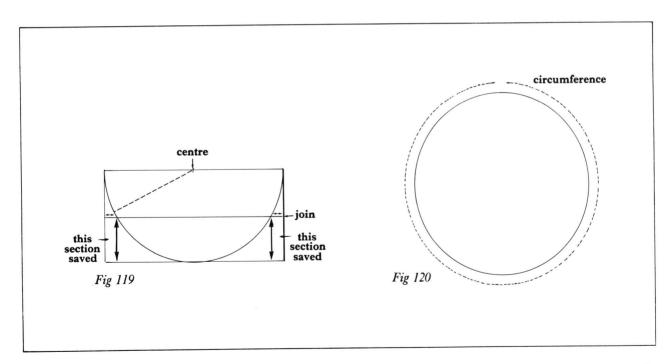

Fig 119

Fig 120

Cut the depth of frill you require (about 15 cm. (6 ins.) is a good average). If it is less than 5 cm. (2 ins.) it tends to stick out, although two layers of this size of frill can look quite effective.

Allow 2.5 cm. (1 in.) for turnings, whatever the depth of frill.

Join all the pieces into a circle and turn the raw edge at the bottom over to the wrong side.

Machine as close to the edge as possible and then trim the fabric right back to the stitch line. (Figure 121)

Press the edge, taking care not to stretch it, and then turn it over once more, so that there is no stitch line showing on the right side. (Figure 122)

Machine right round again close to the edge. You will now have a nice firm edge with one line of stitching showing right at the edge and two lines showing on the wrong side. (Figure 123)

Halve and quarter the frill and mark with pins but do not mark the cloth yet. If the cloth is very large, mark between the quarters at intervals of an eighth of the circumference.

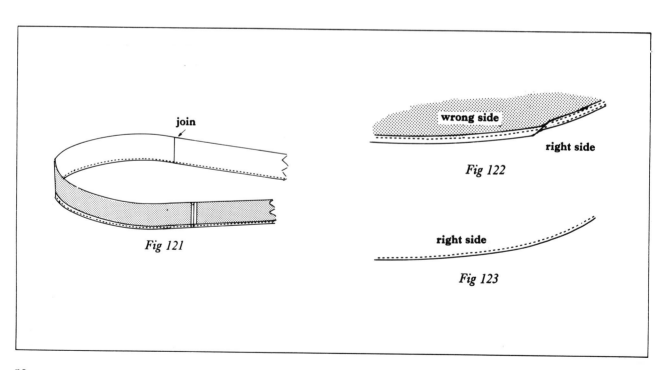

join

Fig 121

wrong side

right side

Fig 122

right side

Fig 123

Gather the frill along the top edge by using a strong thread and zigzag stitching over it (page 9). (Figure 124)

If you cannot work a zigzag stitch on your machine, simply gather each quarter by hand.

Mark a line round the table cover with chalk just *slightly less* than the finished frill measurement. The reason for this is that, as the frill turns back, it takes up a fraction of the fabric and tends to look short.

The table cover must now be halved and quartered on the line just marked as it is less than the circumference of the outer edge.

Pin the frill in place all round the marked line, with the right side of the frill facing the right side of the cloth.

Machine all round, keeping to the line. (Figure 125)

Trim the turning back to 0.7 cm. ($\frac{1}{4}$ in.) and stitch right on the edge of the turning all round again. This will stop the frill from fraying and keep the turning flat. (Figure 126)

Variations of Edgings

Pleated frill – Pleating is very neat and a popular alternative to gathered frills. It does use rather more fabric and takes longer to make but the effect can be quite stunning. (Figure 127)

To pleat on the edge, the cover should be lined so that all the raw edges can be accommodated without bulk.

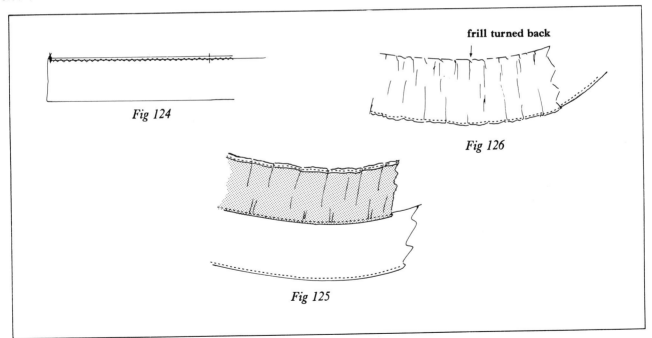

Fig 124

frill turned back

Fig 126

Fig 125

The table cover has to be cut to size, less the depth of the pleat. A turning must be allowed on both the pleat *and* the cover or it will end up shorter than intended.

Decide on the depth of pleat and add turnings of 1.25 cm. (½ in.). Double this measurement to give the cut size.

The number of widths required will vary according to the size of the pleats. Start by pleating up the first 30 cm. (12 ins.) of fabric into the size pleat you require. Now measure the finished length of this sample pleating; if reduced by *half* its original length you will require *twice* times the circumference but if reduced by *one-third* you will need to cut *three* times the circumference.

Cut the necessary number of widths and join in a circle. Fold in half down the length and press the fold. To pleat, fold a section under and machine it in place. Until you become adept at this it would be best to tack the pleats in and check for size before machining.

When the pleating is complete, pin into position on the cloth with the raw edges level and right sides facing. Machine all round.

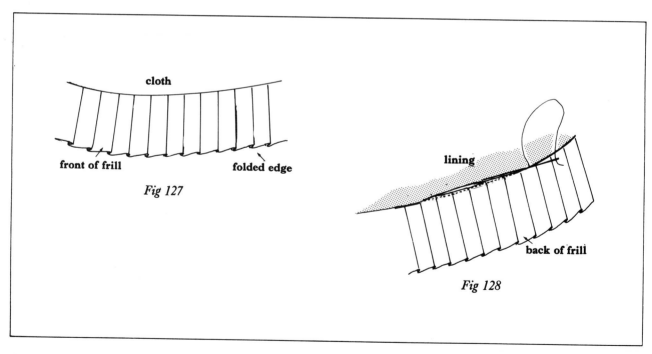

cloth

front of frill   folded edge

Fig 127

lining

back of frill

Fig 128

Cut the lining to the same size as the cloth and, with the pleat turned up, place the lining with its right side facing the fabric.

Pin all round and machine just inside the previous line of stitching, leaving a gap in the machining so that the cloth can be turned inside out.

Turn the cloth right side out, stitch along the gap to make the pleats level, turn in the raw edge and then slip-stitch. (Figure 128)

If the lining moves, catch it with a small, invisible stitch in a couple of places along the join. Generally there is little chance of the lining moving, once the cloth is on the table.

Layered frill – This type of frill is self-descriptive. The lower frill is stitched first and then another placed over it so that about a third of the lower one is left showing. (Figure 129)

Bound-edge – This type can either have the edge of the frill bound before gathering or the actual edge of the cloth can be bound. (Figure 130)

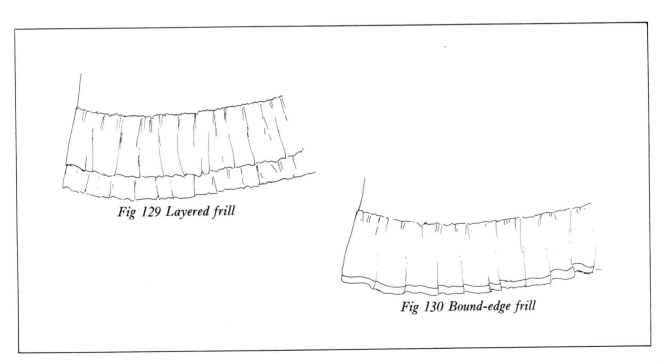

Fig 129 Layered frill

Fig 130 Bound-edge frill

The Oval Table Cover

This type of table cover is not as complicated as it may at first seem.

First make a template of the table top and fold it in half lengthways.

Fold the already joined fabric lengthways and pin the template to it, fold to fold.

Measure out from the edge of the template the depth of the table from the floor at intervals of 15 cm. (6 ins.) and add the hem allowance. You will then be able to cut out your oval table cover with the minimum of trouble. (Figure 131)

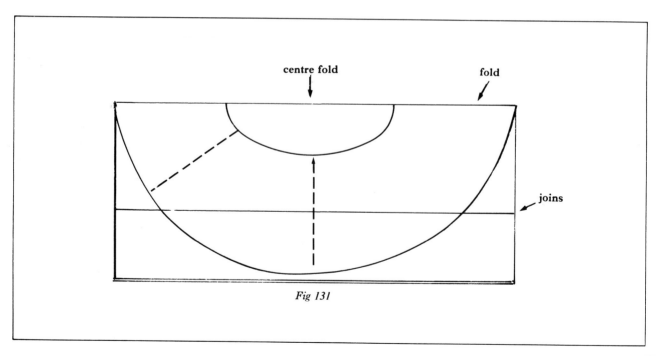

Fig 131

Gathered Table Cover

This type will take a little less fabric. It can be lined or unlined and if you line it the method is the same as for the frilled bedcover. If, however, you prefer it unlined – and therefore easier to wash – the following method is used.

Make a template of the table top, allow turnings and cut to size.

Measure from the top of the table to the floor, allowing 1.25 cm. ($\frac{1}{2}$ in.) turning at the top and 4 cm. ($1\frac{1}{2}$ ins.) for the hem.

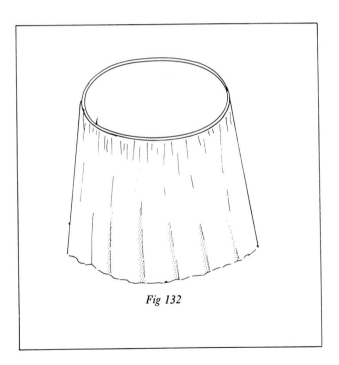

Fig 132

Take the measurement of the circumference of the table top, double it and cut as many widths as you need to cover this amount.

Join the frill widths together in a circle and hem the bottom.

Make up enough piping to pipe round the top circle.

Pipe the circle and then halve and quarter it.

Gather the frill in the same way as the short trimming frills, halve and quarter, and then gather to fit the top. Pin into position and machine to the top circle, as close to the piping as possible.

Even if the frill is unlined, the top would benefit from a lining.

To make this, cut the lining the same size as the table top.

With the table cover right side up and the frill folded in, place the lining on top and pin all round.

Machine nearly all the way round, leaving enough gap to turn the whole thing inside out. Be very careful not to catch the frill in by mistake at this stage, as it is rather bulky.

Turn the right way out and slip-stitch the gap.

Press, fit the cover over the table (Figure 132) and there you are....SUCCESS! !